Somers Commonwealth Immigration Camp

Marina Lutz

Somers Commonwealth Immigration Camp

Memories of Teaching at Victorian School No. 4653 in 1950

Edited by Alice Shore

Somers Commonwealth Immigration Camp: Memories of teaching at Victorian School No. 4653 in 1950
ISBN 978 1 74027 427 2
Copyright © Margarita Volkoff 2007

First published 2007
Reprinted 2021

Ginninderra Press
PO Box 3461 Port Adelaide 5015
www.ginninderrapress.com.au

Contents

Foreword	7
1. Setting the Scene	9
2. The 'New Australians' Arrive	13
3. My Career Begins	19
4. Staffers	23
5. Concerning Food	29
6. George	31
7. Migrants Move On	36
8 Migrants at Work	41
9. Cultural Changes	44
10. I Become a New Australian	48
Postscript	52

Foreword

I met Marina Lutz when she came to join the Barossa Writers in 2002. With talent and enthusiasm, she entered into our writing exercises. Her wit, humanity and friendliness enchanted us all.

Soon after her arrival, Marina read to us a short account of her first year teaching. She had been appointed to a migrant camp, to teach English to the children. That grasped my attention. Here was a woman of unique experience. She was a living piece of Australia's history and I told her that it was important that she write more fully about that camp.

She smiled and confided that she already had. She showed me her manuscript. We discussed ways of improving, reducing and publishing it. Shortly after this, she died, unexpectedly. Her daughter. Margarita Volkoff, found the manuscript and forwarded it to me to edit for submission to Stephen Matthews at Ginninderra Press.

In editing her memoirs I have reduced Marina's writings by about one-third and simplified some of her rather complicated explanations. It is Marina's voice that speaks to us and there were moments when I felt her at my left shoulder as 1 typed. Her story makes engrossing reading. It is, after all, more than a mere historical account. It is a love story on several levels. Enjoy Marina's year at Victorian School No. 4653.

Alice Shore, Birdwood, August 2006

1. Setting the Scene

The war in Europe officially ended in May 1945. After the saturation bombing that had been inflicted over countless months before the final collapse of hostilities, it must have been a relief to those poor souls left to clean up the horrific mess that war causes.

Photographs from that time show piles of rubble where ordinary folk had once lived, worked, relaxed and had their being. No mercy was shown on either side: children, women, the aged were dispossessed of family, home, dreams and belongings. Railways were torn apart; the landscape riddled with scars; communications stopped; families parted. People starved or survived on turnips, morning, noon and night. Cleaning up was done by hand and by those left alive – the women. As well, they had to nourish their children while holding the daily semblance of family life against unimaginable hardships caused by the shortage of every adjunct to normal, civilised living.

That was Europe. The war touched Australians less harshly. We lost brave men. We lost citizens when Darwin was bombed. We had various shortages of food and of building requirements. But we had very little understanding of the totality of the hurt and destruction on the other side of the world: the backbreaking toil that was required by the starving people was beyond our ken.

The Pacific War lasted a few more months. Then two atom bombs wiped out two more cities and untold thousands of ordinary human beings. When it was all over, we blithely tried to continue our lives as they had been before 1939, a life of reproducing the colonial counterpart of British culture. Going to Britain was often referred to as 'going home'. We had Dominion status, under the Statute of Westminster, from the 1920s, and we seemed not to mind our lower status. World

War II was the catalyst of change: our boys gave their life blood for the 'Mother country' on far battlefields once again.

When Japan entered the war, Australia was isolated. Our imports were curtailed. Our exports were limited to war needs. We were thrown onto our own resources. Our men enlisted for overseas.

Women were now needed in factories and on farms. We accepted the war effort, assuming that the war would end some time, the men would come home and life would continue as before.

Australians were mostly egalitarian. We lived simply, aiming to own our own home. We worked a forty-eight-hour week and kept the Sabbath holy – more or less. Mail was delivered twice a day and on Saturday mornings. Tradesmen delivered milk, bread, vegetables and groceries, and ice in summer, to the back door.

Banks opened Mondays to Fridays from 10 a.m. to 3 p.m. We had not heard of credit unions nor of building societies.

On Sundays decent people went to church. In some houses there was no work, not even embroidery. Families would gather around the piano or reed organ and sing, preferably hymns, or read instructive literature. Sundays were dull. Married women were generally not employed: the husband was expected to be the bread winner. There were long engagements as newly weds were expected to have a house ready to move into. As these were pre-Pill days, chastity was important. Although our life was not easy, it was pleasant enough. There was routine. There were mores. There was stability.

The war changed all that. The men enlisted – again – to serve their King. Patriotism was strong. Women who didn't go into the workforce knitted for 'our boys', raised money for the Red Cross, served at the Comforts Fund, Open House, Toc H. There were sporadic air raid exercises and Prayer Days of Intercession. We had some form of rationing of tea, sugar, butter, clothing, dress materials and petrol. Cars were put on blocks to await the war's end, though few people owned cars then, as excellent public transport served the cities. Some unions went on strike for more money while most workers generally tried to save on money and materials for the war effort: "our boys' were struggling in appalling conditions to protect our freedom. There were coal shortages. Trains were restricted. We had gas rationing. Occasionally an elderly person died when they tried to use the gas, found it didn't work and forgot to switch off the tap.

Suffering for those whose 'boys' would never return was real. But for the majority of us the war was a far-off event, in other lands and of other ideologies. Once peace had come again, we would simply pick up the threads of life and continue as before.

Peace brought more changes than one could ever envisage. Our newspapers gave us accounts of the millions of displaced persons in Europe who could not return to their homes. They had been tossed like autumn leaves in uncertain winds. No one knew what to do with these twelve million poor lost souls. Twelve million was about our total population then. We were xenophobic. There were small pockets of foreigners here and there: Germans in the Barossa Valley, Chinese in goldmining towns like Bendigo or among the Broome pearl divers. But they never upset the tenor of our lives. We lived as close as possible to British mores and that meant enforcing these onto people from other lands.

For some, the prospect of all those foreigners coming in and taking our homes, our jobs from us was too daunting a fate. A propaganda exercise was mounted to allay our fears: the twelve million were not to sweep down upon us, for our government would implement a screening process. A select few would be allowed in and we were to welcome them in true freedom and peace. Those found not worthy of having our largesse would not be allowed to enter. With the White Australia policy we could deny them on all sorts of pretexts. Although most of Australia's early settlers were of convict extraction, with the exception of South Australia, these latter-day settlers had to be 'worthy' of adoption. They had to be healthy, especially they had to be free of tuberculosis, and white.

Our government decided to bring in the newcomers as workers.

They were to build up our economy after the loss of men in the war. They were under contract for two years and could be sent to wherever labour was needed. Male migrants were designated as labourers while females were domestics, regardless of the background or education of each migrant. It was a very short-sighted policy. In bringing these poor, homeless, stateless people to our shores, Australia made an economic investment in humans to build up the country with a good, white population. Humanitarian ideals were a few paces behind.

The first shiploads were chosen to be appealing. Good-looking 'Nordic' types, they gave a good impression to the not-always-willing hosts. It was thought they would be better accepted than the earlier Jewish refugees who had arrived before the war, and Muslims who did not look British. The newspapers of the day made much of the first arrivals, complete with captivating photos of the happy faces of our new citizens.

From the migrants' point of view, Australia was about as far as anyone could go on the planet to be away from the misery of Europe. They had lost virtually everything that they held dear. Some had even lost their names and nationalities. Stateless, they had no passports, merely a small piece of paper permitting them to come ashore in Australia. Many knew as much about Australia as Australia knew about them, which was precious little. Both parties were, like it or not, launched on a great learning curve.

2. The 'New Australians' Arrive

While I was at teachers' college in 1949, the Victorian Education *Gazette* began advertising vacancies for teachers at migrant camps.

Teachers with a knowledge of French and German were needed to teach English and the Australian Way of Life to the arriving migrants, now referred to as 'new Australians'. Accommodation was provided at the camps. Offering an unusual outlet, the advertisements fired my imagination. It offered something different from the customary one-teacher school placement. That I did not relish.

Our one-year training course was designed to fit us to teach at any primary school level anywhere in the state. We learned how to teach every subject on the curriculum, handle teachers, inspectors, outer offices and the Department and how to cope with emergencies.

My fellow teachers in training had been student teachers for one or two years prior to entry into the teachers' college. That meant that we had been dogsbodies, doing odd jobs around the school as well as within the classroom. Ruling up pages for the young ones, tying their shoelaces and hair ribbons, hearing them read and taking charge of a class filled in our time.

Sometimes we would give a demonstration lesson, which was criticised by the class teacher. These crit. lessons were used to judge our latent teaching abilities. By the time we were admitted into teachers' college we had already had some practical experience. We were guaranteed employment at the end of our very arduous college year. After college, new teachers were posted by the Department to a one-teacher, or rural, school. One could nominate a school, but no one believed they would be sent there.

College was stimulating. The student body was a happy lot. Some were returned servicemen.

At the end of the year, I was offered an extension, quite an honour. It meant study at the university, a degree and teaching at secondary level. Three times I refused this offer. My chances of being appointed to a migrant camp were very slim. But it was worth a try, and try I did. I was appointed to Somers Commonwealth Immigration Camp.

What did I know about migrants and migrant camps? Largely nothing, except that they were often called Balts because, we were told, they came from the Baltic countries. No one knew where to find them on a map. Of refugees we did know a little . They were called 'refos', dumped in suburbs such as Carlton and St Kilda and treated with some distaste.

The new arrivals were of a different order. Some people were sympathetic to their plight, while others saw them as a threat.

Newspapers published photos of faces happy with excited anticipation of their new life in a free country far from war and its terrible toll. Articles were written with details of individuals. We were to understand more about these citizens.

The first requirement was accommodation. The wartime military bases were recycled as migration reception centres or migrant holding centres. The former were simply to shelter the arrivals until they were assigned to their work places, such as with the Snowy Mountains scheme, or until they went on to a holding centre, where they could stay for up to six months. By then they were expected to have found work and accommodation elsewhere.

There was no lack of employment and if one found a job uncongenial, one merely found another.

Camp accommodation was Spartan. Thrown up in wartime to be used as army or air force training camps, there were no frills of any kind. After the war, as temporary accommodation for an itinerant people, there was no point in making things so comfortable that no one would want to move on. A shortage of building materials continued well after the war's end. This was the time when we had to do without verandas. There were sad stories of people queuing up at the former home of someone deceased and wanting to acquire the accommodation immediately. The Australian dream of owning one's own home was a nightmare. The New Australians with no money, no resources and no contacts came last in the race to be housed. Some people in the holding centres stayed longer than the allotted six months.

Very few of the migrants had any knowledge of English. As so many were 'Balts', their geographical distance from English-speaking countries and the poverty of so many even in peaceful times in their own countries would have precluded such learning.

When they were overrun during the war, German or Russian was foisted upon them.

The Department required us teachers to have a knowledge of French and German. No French-speaking migrants came to the camp and the German was DP Deutsch, a pidgin German. It became the lingua franca of migrant camps.

At that time, there must have been difficulty in finding teachers who spoke other languages willing to teach in a camp. I had been fortunate enough to attend a high school where German and French were in the curriculum. I had also learned Latin and, later, Japanese, making me an 'odd bod'.

Remembering that we were an outpost of the British Empire and that the British are xenophobic, one understands that we were language shy. The Department had to find teachers willing to take on the task of teaching our language to the newcomers, especially to the young.

In the camp were some school buildings where the servicemen had been taught. Small classrooms, equipped with blackboards, three to a hut, were connected by doors through internal walls.

When we, the new staff, arrived at the camp, that is what we found, plus a few boxes of chalk.

Finally, my stubbornness paid off and my appointment was made legal. I was to go to Somers CIC, beyond Frankston, which was, at that time, the end of the line. Somers was in the middle of farmland with the waters of Port Phillip Bay on one side, a picturesque setting. For most of the year it was sleepy, coming to life in the summer only. Possibly the secluded location was ideal for an RAAF training camp. Sometime after the war it was converted into a holiday camp. The huts were jollied up a bit with paint which slowly faded when the Department took over. The camp was right on the seafront, with only a small line of shrubs to protect it from winds that blew across the bay. Some distance away was a hamlet which boasted a shop cum kiosk. Further away was the tiny town of Nestings. We came to know both the hamlet and Nestings.

There was no public transport. Once we had arrived by train at Frankston, the remaining section had to be covered by our initiative, or by the camp bus. Few people had their own car. After the war One had to wait on a list for a car.

The electric train from Flinders Street was a pleasant trip lasting just over an hour. The stretch between Frankston and Somers could be a mystery tour with signage lacking and then not entirely reliable.

The camp buildings were laid out in rows, with the school buildings at the northern end. In the small space in front stood a flagpole. On the eastern side was a hut which was set aside as living quarters for the teaching staff. The headmaster, one half of the staff and one of the adult educators shared these quarters. In the centre of the camp, and on the main road, was the office. The administration staff, who worked here, were housed in quarters nearby. On the opposite side of the main road stood the recreation hut, with the mess hall behind that. Not far away was the staff mess, with the kitchen between the two messes. Around this main area were scattered the living quarters of the migrants, with cold and draughty bathrooms, open at the top. Removed from the hurly burly of the camp proper was the hospital, a busy place nevertheless.

The camp director lived somewhat remotely on the southern rim, abutting onto what was allocated to the rest of the staff. I believe that our quarters had been officers' quarters formerly. Within our hut, the head of adult education and his wife lived at the eastern end. Two smaller rooms, an open area which led to three more rooms and a small washroom cum shower and toilet made this one of the more desirable living huts.

Those allocated to the migrants were more basic. Of about ten feet each way, no doubt they had been built as mere sleeping areas. But now they housed a family per room – Mama, Papa (if he was not working away from camp) and however many children.

Luckily most families were not large. Yet it was not an ideal arrangement. Single men were housed separately, away from married persons' quarters.

MELBOURNE, C.2,
16th January, 1950

Appointment of Temporary Assistant

Memorandum for—

M iss Beverley M. Lutz-Dyer,
St. Margarets,
224 King Street,
BENDIGO.

I have to inform you that you have been appointed to the position of Temporary Assistant at School No. 4653, Somers Camp ~~during the absence of Mr.~~ pending the appointment of a permanent assistant.

You should take up duty there on the 31st January, 1950.

As soon as you commence duty at this school you should complete the attached form and forward it, through the Head Teacher, to the District Inspector.

You are ~~are not~~ entitled to claim travelling expenses.

If travelling expenses are payable you may submit, subject to the prescribed conditions, a claim for such expenses on the attached L. 2a. form. A reference to these conditions appears in the notes at the end of the list of vacancies in primary schools advertised in the current issue of the *Education Gazette*. These conditions must be strictly adhered to.

Secretary

3. My Career Begins

We were ready to begin our careers in this out-of-the-way place when the school year began. It turned out that I was the only one who actually wanted to be appointed to a migrant camp. Even before the term had officially started, some admitted they wanted to be transferred away. We were eight young girls, fresh from college, with one young man and the headmaster. The other seven girls had been to the same teachers' college in Melbourne and thus knew each other. I had been to a smaller, country college at Bendigo. The young man had some few years of teaching experience already. He kept to himself, outnumbered by females.

Short, tubby, balding and bespeckled, the headmaster appeared somewhat affable. Rather fussy, he flattered us. Perhaps he was in his early fifties. He drove a coupé and liked to take us around the area in the first days after our arrival. As eight girls in one coupé was uncomfortable we gradually declined his offers and stayed in our rooms to simply prepare the next day's work.

Our classes were small. We had no inkling how to teach English and the Australian Way of Life. We had nothing but a few of our own books and our 'aids' which we had prepared not really knowing where to begin. The school was furnished with blackboards, chalk and one duster between two rooms. Plus the children. We'd had no special training. It was sink or swim.

The children were delightful. Some had picked up a few phrases of English. It was impossible to teach as in a standard state school. Some had had a little schooling in the DP camps in Europe. Others were illiterate in their own tongues. Just like children everywhere, some were good and some were wicked little imps. We came to love them all, making the best of the situation. Teaching children sufficient words so that an intelligent conversation was possible required much patience on both sides and gave laughter as well as mistakes. The achievement of comprehension gave joy to both sides. If for no other reason, this teaching showed immediate results coming from the teachers' efforts and dedication to the class and to each child individually. Successes were gratifying, becoming our guidelines, which grew into our modus operandi.

The headmaster was of very little help. We never saw him take a class. He fussed around with pieces of paper on which we were to make lists of this and that. The results we never saw. In the beginning, in answer to our problems, he would say that he 'would fix it. And so he became known among us as 'Mr Fixit'. We decided that he must be one of those teachers not bad enough to actually be sacked and not good enough to be in the classroom. He probably spent his career being shunted from one posting to another, succeeding nowhere. This was how he had come to be headmaster in this small and unimportant outpost.

To grade the children was not easy and he tried various methods, none satisfactory. By age was one method. But individuals varied.

Their knowledge of English was not much of a guide as to their abilities in maths, for example. No sooner would we have some semblance of order than a fresh intake would descend on us and we had to start all over again. Some of the brightest were among the first to leave camp when Papa found outside work and accommodation.

Fourteen or sixteen in a class formed out highest number. The teaching had to be particular. There could be fourteen languages and dialects in the room. Thus progress was quite slow. There was no one to show us a method better than the ones we devised for ourselves. The lower classes were easier for the teacher. The older children had had some grounding in German schools before they arrived here and were frustrated at not being able to communicate freely.

Their dedication to learning surprised us all. We were accustomed to casual Australian children. The formal behaviour of camp children was another culture shock. Once we realised how well they had been brought up at home, we were delighted when the older boys, asked to show their work, would jump from their desks, click their heels together and bow from the waist.

This behaviour did not endure for long. One evening as I was going up to the mess hut for the evening meal, one of my class came running by. I waved at her. To my surprise she stopped running, dropped me a curtsey and then ran on. It cured me from being too casual.

In class we spoke s-l-o-w-l-y and c-l-e-a-r-l-y to the children so that they could better hear each syllable and sound. Hopefully the clear enunciation would give understanding. With accuracy in their own language, they gave each sound its full value. Their English was delightful to hear as their vocabularies grew.

Every six weeks a new intake would arrive and Mr Fixit would flurry with his papers. Classes would be shaken up and all of us would go back to learning new names, filling out another class register, trying to assess the level of language of the newcomers – if they had any English at all – and giving them confidence.

To us teachers, the formal paperwork that the Department required seemed a waste of time. But not for Mr Fixit. He had an unending supply of forms. To our silent amusement, many of his pieces of paper seemed to have come from a preserving company: they were the right size and shape to fit a jam jar, with one surface a shining yellow. No one could ever sort out the attendance figures required by the Department: the constant movement of children from one class to another at Mr Fixit's request made figures unfathomable. Their removal from the camp school into Australian schools would have defied an Einstein.

We wondered whether the figures mattered at all. There was no truancy. Everyone in the camp knew everyone else in their language group, each a hotbed of gossip. The parents respected learning, encouraging their children to attend the school. I believe the children enjoyed coming to us. We went to a lot of time and trouble to make learning interesting to them.

We staffers were permitted to use the camp bus which went into Frankston Saturday mornings. We could buy glossy magazines from which we then cut pictures. These we pasted onto cardboard and labelled, as in ordinary kindergarten and first grades. After all, there is a limit to how much explanation the waving of hands can do. It is an old truism that a picture is worth a thousand words. When I introduced a new word [I would hear an undercurrent of many tongues explaining it to the slower children. To learn a foreign language at any age is a huge task. For these children, who were expected to be quickly assimilated into ordinary Australian classes, it was imperative that they learn as quickly as possible.

The children dressed in the children's fashion of the day, Continental style. They preferred bright colours and knitted garments, so different from what 'old Australians' wore. The little girls had plaits of curious design. Some wore an unusual crown of plaits circling the head. On special occasions some would be dressed in national costume. We gasped at the intricate patterns, lovingly and painstaking handmade; the beautiful headdresses with flowing ribbons and the fancy shirts worn by the boys. All was new to us. We were impressed and we came to realise that national dress was as important to them as a tartan is to a Scot.

I found the children a joy. They gave something to teaching which I am sure none of us would have found elsewhere – that is, they had an eagerness to absorb all that we could impart in a delightful formal way. It was not submissive. It was respectful. They gave us teachers credit for the service we gave to them. This made me acutely aware of the difference in our backgrounds and | reflected, with dismay, the contrary attitude of my countrymen with an apathy to raising personal standards and the lack of a love of learning for its own sake.

4. Staffers

Other staffers worked in administration, hospital, transport and canteen.

As the hospital was removed from the camp, we rarely saw the hospital staffers. Occasionally we glimpsed them in the mess hall, sitting apart from others. Most working in transport were mature men. Whether they had their wives with them I cannot remember.

Since they were on call for all, they kept odd hours. Mostly we noticed the ambulance racing off to the Frankston Hospital for another very new Australian to join society. Government propaganda at that time was 'populate or perish' and populate they did. Since there was no other way of going into Frankston, the camp bus was like a taxi service. From there we could catch a train into the city.

The bus also took believers, both Anglican and Catholic, to church at the Flinders Naval Depot. When the men working outside the camp came back on weekends, the bus picked them up from the railway station. The bus returned them on Sunday evenings, bringing back to camp those staffers who had enjoyed a weekend away.

The staff in the adult education section were employees of the Commonwealth Government. The head of the section was a gentleman retired from a South Australian private school. He lived in our hut with his wife. Both kept a kindly eye on us girls. We called him 'Boss' and his wife 'Mrs Boss', with more affection than given to our own head.

In our hut was also a maiden lady of uncertain age and strange ways. She attracted a following of young men. The terms 'patience' or 'aesthetic' with exaggerated poetic qualities suited them. Many years later I heard that she was declared a national treasure when she turned one hundred in Japan and that, aged 104, she 'came out'. A Welsh lady lived in the other hut, at the far end of the camp, with the other girls. Of retirement age, she was pleasant to chat with. She had little in common with us girls. She kept very much to herself, fulfilling her teaching duties.

In contrast, the youngest member of the adult education staff was a fair-haired, rather scruffy-looking man. He seemed to be constantly down-at-heel. George was popular with his classes and he lived in the single men's quarters, along with the kitchen staff and one or two office staff. The canteen manager, an Irish man, managed to supply the migrants with little extras, as though he ran a general store. The business was done via the children as interpreters. How they managed with his strong Irish idiom one never knew. He spoke no English as such.

A few migrants were employed among the office staff. They were not happily received by the Australians working there. The liaison Officer was a man of Latvian origin. His Herculean task was to sort out the various misunderstandings that arose between administration and migrants, between one staff and another, between migrant and migrant. They often brought old hatreds and prejudices with them. He had to restore peace in all encounters. He was a perfect gentleman and I heard that he had been the chancellor of the exchequer in his home country. The sad part is that, when he left the camp, he would become a chicken farmer or milk bar attendant. All his expertise in PR work was wasted, simply because he had no British qualifications. Such was the fate of our best migrants, an unforgivable loss to our country caused by the government. A story repeated countless times, it should make Australians hang their head in shame.

The liaison officer had a flat, of two or three rooms, within camp, a real luxury. He had with him not only his wife and three children, but also his wife's sister. What intrigued me was that Mum spoke German, Tante Maria spoke Russian and Papa used Latvian. Before they set a foot in our school, the children were fluent in three languages.

One day, he remarked to me, 'My people are dark.' I thought to myself, Yes, a lot of mine appear to be dark also. His 'darks' were the lesser-educated, while in mine 'darkness' was just plain bigotry and ignorance. One saw this in the behaviour of the office staff dealing daily with mundane matters with the migrants. We often thought that patience was singularly lacking. I often wondered how the managers would have managed if the positions were reversed and they were forced by circumstances to live in a far-off country and to speak a foreign language. Would they have done as well as these poor migrants? They forgot that twelve miles out to sea they would be classed as migrants too.

The staffers found it amusing when a migrant would ask for 'soup' instead of 'soap', or that when an Aussie asked for 'a box of matches' they would put up their fists for a spar. The Australian who misunderstood the migrant's misunderstandings soon had a right royal problem on his hands and I marvelled how the Latvian man constantly sorted out differences.

A Hungarian girl worked in the office. In her mid-twenties, she was considered to be 'fast', not desirable in those puritan days. She and I struck up an acquaintance. I thought she was sophisticated, far beyond my experience, an interesting person. We passed many pleasant off duty hours together, both being considered 'odd bods', me because I came from a college different from the other girls and she because of her ill-founded reputation.

At first I had been quite lonely. I was different, not only because I had trained at another college, but also because I was the only one of the girls who had come willingly to the camp and thus did not join in with their loud lamentations about this their first appointment. Later they were very happy to be working in the camp and rose to the challenges offered with enthusiasm and verve. They knew each other from the days of their studies and did not share my interest in languages.

Marguerite and I formed a bond through many small interests. She told me small snippets of camp gossip, with a wicked sense of humour. For her office co-workers she had scant respect and took delight in satirising the Australians with their narrow views of how women should comport themselves. One of those men assured me one day that Marguerite wore only two items of clothing. I assumed he must have looked very carefully to be sure of his facts.

The kitchen staff and cleaners had little contact with us. Some of the girls went walking with kitchen helpers and joined in their entertainment in camp. There was nothing serious.

All in all, our staff of eight young girls was the youngest group in camp. We were dedicated to our employment. We were probably the most carefree, absorbed with our little charges and the excitement from this interesting teaching.

All of the various staffers went about their daily tasks in their own ways. We met together in the mess hall at meal times. We girls had most in common with the office staff, especially with the young ones. Some of them sat at our table and joined in with chatter and banter. We were in the same interesting and challenging situation, different from work outside the little world that the camp became for us.

Staff at Somers C.I.C. 1950

Pupils at Somers C.I.C. 1950

5. Concerning Food

Food was the greatest cause of complaint and unrest in camp.

We girls all came from similar middle-class backgrounds, used to the standard meat and three veg of Aussie cuisine at that time.

Beef was served as the main meal, sometimes lamb. Vegetables were, of course, boiled for that was the way our forebears had eaten them, boiled to death. It was the custom to bake the meat on Sunday, have it as stew on Mondays, maybe the chops on Tuesdays, fried on Wednesdays, and so on. Not very exciting, this was good "British cooking'. It was good. Eat it all up. It is hard to imagine the differences between what we eat nowadays and what we ate fifty years ago.

Camp food was beyond all imaginings. No nationality could, nor would, own it. It was simply not edible. It was constantly awful, always looking like plodge and drowned in some sort of greasy gravy that ringed the plates with a reddish ring of paprika.

Until then, most of us had a vague idea that paprika was an Hungarian condiment.

Day after day, the same mess, whether goulash or stew, stew or goulash, was presented to us. There must have been some variation on this theme but it escapes my memory. If that was what was served at the staff mess, then, heavens, what did the migrants have to put up with?

Eventually, we teachers sent our meals back and asked for toast, which we spread with Vegemite. In those days, the Vegemite lids carried the slogan 'A mere smear will suffice'. Our witty ones named it 'mere smear'. Then came a directive that teachers ask for only toast at breakfast. We were obliged to stick to the menu or starve. We did wonder which was the lesser of the two evils.

No one knew who was the chef. Perhaps he hid his identity for his safety. Migrant men were employed in the kitchens, mostly single men who I suspect had never seen a saucepan, let alone instructions of what to do with it. If the food we were served was a sort of experiment, then the plan needed to go back to the drawing board, or to Mrs Beaton.

The situation was worse for the migrants. Unused to eating lamb, many of them became ill.

At one time in camp a riot broke out against the food that was being served. To an Australian, the meal looked like good meat.

What an ungrateful lot these migrants were. Very few of the Australians then had any idea of the other non-British foods available in city markets. Some of these came easily available after the arrival of the Jews and in the areas of the German colonists, like in the Barossa Valley with its mixture of sausages. Chinese cafés existed in main cities. But few people patronised them, apart from Chinese and a few itinerants passing by and sailors, certainly not 'decent folk'.

The advent in Australia of a demand for foreign food was arguably the best part of the migration program: the migrants found work and acquired houses, became part of our lifestyle, merging into the mainstream of Australian life. The revolution in our ways of eating is permanent and vital. We now know about veal and pork, which we didn't before. Once, chicken was something of a rarity and expensive at 12 shillings and 6 pence while the weekly wage was about £4 or £5. Chicken is now commonplace. Those condiments we rarely heard of are now readily available, from Asia as well as Europe. Vegetables like the courgette or zucchini, of which we had never heard, are now as common as the old spud. Instead of the rigid and limited menus once normal, Australians have now found the adventure of cooking. We are able to grow almost everything in our wonderful climates and have tasted the difference between what the colonists had and what the migrants have taught us to enjoy.

6. George

As the weeks and months rolled on, life in camp followed a gentle routine. It was pleasant and easy enough: meals were provided, our rooms were cleaned for us. Teaching was interesting and challenging, giving us girls the independence with wages we sought.

After school, we would walk together in the local area. Acquaintances evolved into friendships. Before long, we were joined by escorts from the kitchen staff, or perhaps one or two of the office staff...and George, as scruffy as ever, but proving to be good company. It was carefree and blithe company. We were fancy free and enjoying the moment.

The kitchenmen, whatever their background, treated us with respect. They probably learned English faster than others. Some of the office were Australian. One, with excellent English, was Latvian. He had the bonus of his own language as well as some German. Like many, he had endured hard times before coming to Australia, though he preferred not to speak about it. He and George, being of similar age, were good friends.

Films were screened on Saturday nights in one of the hamlets nearby. Occasionally, some of our group would go. Autumn turned into winter and the winds became even colder. We preferred to stay where it was warmer, at a singalong in the hall at which almost the whole camp took part. Words of songs were shown on a screen and a pointer kept the singers up to the right word. What the migrants made of 'Daisy, Daisy', 'Shine on, harvest moon', 'Row, row, row your boat' and the like I don't know.

We sat in the darkened hall and sang with gusto, having a good time. It was lots of fun for us, but bewilderment for the newcomers as Mr Boss, perhaps he was peeved that we preferred the company of the younger men to his hospitality in his coupé. At the time we were unaware that he disapproved of any fraternisation, however innocent. However, this was not immediately obvious. We kept company as a large group, fluctuating in number day by day.

Nothing serious happened. So Mr Fixit was on the wrong track.

I had my twentieth birthday early in the first term. In honour of the occasion, George stole flowers from the director's garden and presented them to me. Everyone thought it was a bit of a joke.

Some time later, George invited me to go to a film with the group.

I refused because I did not want to be seen with a down-at-heel escort. Then, some time after this, one of the girls said, 'George came into mess for a meal and he's had a haircut.' This was big news. I thought it was one of the camp jokes until I saw him. He looked almost civilised. The girls found out that he was Russian and that he had recently suffered the loss of his mother in sad circumstances. At first I did not believe that he was Russian. They were black of eye and beard and sang melancholy songs. He spoke like an Australian, slouched like an Australian and passed as a local boy from way back.

To find facts, one must go to the source. So I asked him if this was all true. Was he – unbelievably – Russian? To my great surprise he admitted it, stating details of his birth at Harbin in Manchuria and that he had come to Australia when he was eleven. To my next question, 'Do you speak Russian?' he answered, 'Yes.' That changed everything. Here was a language not taught in school. I could look intelligent about Harbin. It had come into some of our college lectures the previous year. Here was someone who called it home. All of a sudden, George and I had a common interest to talk about. He proved to be an interesting companion. The next time he invited me out with him, I accepted. He began to smarten up a little. We reached a compromise.

Once, we all decided to attend a local dance. We set out cross country in walking shoes. We girls carried our dancing slippers in bags and lifted up our dresses as we stepped over rough places.

The locals did not relish our company. So we girls were left to ourselves and when the dance was over, we tramped back to camp the way we had come, brogues on feet, dance shoes in our hands. It was the first and last time we patronised a local dance.

One deep winter night, someone organised a dance in the recreation hut. Here many of us spent off-duty hours, playing board games or cards or just talking and socialising. There were tables and chairs, possibly table tennis equipment. There was nothing smart, for our needs were simple and we found entertainment and amusement in ways which today would be classed as childish. We made out own fun and had many laughs at the little day-to-day events around us. We had records and a wind-up gramophone. There was a keg of beer to ease our thirst. Where it came from I do not know. It was a tasty beer and I was not a beer drinker. No one got drunk or unmannerly. We simply enjoyed ourselves, simply. Fully.

What amused me at that time was the fact that the other girls, from decent and sheltered backgrounds, had never had former contact with the demon drink. This weekly keg of beer may have been their first essay into 'fast living', incredible as it is to us today. They could consider themselves very modern and daring in their sampling the drink; none smoked, nor drank hard liquor, and drugs were unheard of. We were not bored because we did not have the vanity of mind that leads to boredom.

Once again I was the odd bod. I had been taught at home from the age of twelve how to drink an occasional glass of wine at the table if guests were present. Beer was drunk at home on days above the century. Cold beer. We had brandy in the house as a cure-all and to this day I still regard brandy as a medicine.

So I knew the demon drink as a friend, as most Europeans would.

But I soon became labelled as a 'scarlet woman – she drinks, you know'. Moreover, the girls learned faster than me that a little wine is indeed a pleasant thing. By the end of the second term, the girls were sampling red wine by the tumbler in the single men's quarters and coming back quite late at night and full of giggles.

We enjoyed all the dances: the Pride of Erin, foxtrot, modern waltz and the like. It soon became obvious that George was a good dancer.

The Sunday evening dances were good fun and if we were in camp on Sundays, which we usually were, then dance we would.

Life in camp was a bowl of cherries as the saying goes and should have continued as such, but for Mr Fixit. It appeared that he had friends in the Department who had ears that heard his voice.

When we left camp for the first term vacation, going to our various homes, mine the furthest away, we knew that one girl would not be returning. She had asked for a transfer which had been granted to her. However, when I reached home, there waiting for me was a transfer to a one-teacher school just out of Ballarat. I was greatly puzzled and thought that it was a mistake. After all, I had asked to be sent to a camp. The others had come under sufferance. There had been no complaint against me, as far as I knew, about my work.

The more we discussed it at home, the more I could not understand why I had to be moved. Mother cautioned me to be silent and to go back to camp as usual on the same train from the city as the others would take. She then went immediately to the Education Department to find out the facts. My mother was a formidable redhead, not to be faced lightly in battle. If only the Department pen-pushers had known.

When we met together in the rail carriage on the return trip, there was a young man who declared, 'I'm to replace a female who's to be replaced.' Shock and horror. The girls looked at each other and saw that our full complement was on board. They wondered.

I confided in George but no one else and waited for Mother to telephone and explain. It turned out that Mr Fixit had complained that I had been to the single men's quarters, drinking with them.

We decided that he had named only me because of my friendship with George. The other girls had no special escorts. To Mr Fixit my fraternisation was taboo.

As soon as I knew the reason for my transfer and it had all been sorted out, I was reinstated. I told the other girls who 'the girl to be transferred' was. It changed some attitudes and at the end of that term Mr Fixit was himself replaced by a married headmaster who came with his wife and proved to be a good and caring head, greatly respected by his little staff. By then I had asked for a transfer at the end of the year. I regretted this once I knew that Mr Fixit was to be transferred.

Ironically, the majority of the girls stayed on at camp longer than I who had asked for the position. The situation showed that fraternisation was not desirable to some. Their reason ran like this: the migrants are foreign, their ways foreign, we did not fight two world wars to be overrun by foreigners. Teach them our language and way of life. And keep apart.

In many ways our situation had altered. Mr Fixit had been found out, my growing relationship with George had been spotlighted unnecessarily and the other girls had been given a warning about being too light-hearted with the kitchenmen lest this be misunderstood. We became more circumspect in our innocent friendships.

Mr Fixit had done no one any service and a great deal of harm to himself. The replacement young man was himself replaced in term three by a very pleasant young man who proved popular with future staff.

At the end of the next year, 1951, George and I married. My mother was distressed, ironically as she had been headstrong in her decision to marry my father of German descent. She tried to make our marriage miserable. Another story.

In marriage I gained a foreign name and, although Australian born and bred, was sometimes treated as an outsider. George had been naturalised before taking up teaching with the Adult Education Department. We both were equally Aussie. I was well accepted among the Russian community. Deciding to learn Russian, I received a lot of help from the Russians with whom we associated. I was treated as one of the family. Not so among my own family.

Beforehand my love of languages had been applauded. To be trying to learn my husband's tongue was almost a sin. Mother deplored my association with the Russians whom she met. In the end I learned to separate my life into two compartments – former family ways and new Russian ways. And never the twain shall meet.

7. Migrants Move On

Australia is a harsh land, hard, difficult, demanding. But to those who survive, it is rewarding and infinitely beautiful. It was both hard to settle and hard to settle into. The first settlers came under duress and were forced to tame an unknown quantity. Somehow, they coped. Later those who came freely, as in South Australia, still had hard times. However, they too coped and built a free country which later generations developed to world standing as an entity in its own right. In serving the parent Empire with the libation of young men's blood in overseas wars for Europe, it gained dignity and honour.

There is nothing easy in the process of giving up the country of one's birth and going to live in another country where there are new customs, new ways, and perhaps a new tongue to learn and master. The fibres of one's being remain the roots of one's traditions and there is always a Sehnsucht, or yearning, for those roots.

For some who never have a chance to return to their roots there is loneliness and alienation. Those who have the chance to return may feel distress at finding change all about them in the homeland with the landmarks of their youth swept away by progress.

The migrants who came to our land after World War II broke new ground in many ways. Such an influx had not been seen here since the goldrush days of the 1850s. So many new tongues to contend with; so little real preparation for them; so much suffering to contend with as DPs; so much discomfort of a different kind to be faced. It is not surprising that many of the newcomers could not survive the first few very hard years in this harsh country, among some very hard-hearted locals. It is small wonder that some migrants gave up the struggle, drank too much, lost their reason and perhaps took their own lives.

Those who coped better have mostly become Australian while retaining the hopes and fears of their birth land. Their children are Australian born and may or may not have great knowledge of the lands of their parents. All are contributors to a stronger and hopefully more tolerant Australia.

The 'new Australian' arrivals of the 1940s and 1950s travelled by sea on a five-week voyage. Many left from the port of Naples, embarking on ships that had been requisitioned by the government for this purpose. The quality of the voyage varied depending on the standard of food, shipboard conditions and provision of English lessons. The travellers were poor, with no money to spend on the trifles that tourists buy as mementos. The ships did not provide the entertainment of cruise ships. Many complained of boredom on the long voyage.

Usually, the sexes were segregated, wives and children apart from husbands and fathers. This arrangement continued after landfall. It was done to ease accommodation and in many cases applied to camp life, no doubt to speed up the migrants' resolve to find their own accommodation. At Somers, families had their own quarters, humble, cramped and sparse.

On arrival at whichever port they were to disembark, the arrivals were taken to a reception centre by bus or train or even by trucks with a few benches in the back. The rail cars provided were definitely third-class, for comfort was not the first priority and Australia was still suffering from postwar shortages of materials and manpower. Any means sufficed to take the arrivals from the ports to a camp. From Melbourne to Bonegilla could take up to ten hours and the culture shock must have been enormous.

Once they reached their destinations, there were beds and food. The beds may have been mere army cots with old army blankets and food in abundance. One woman who had arrived as a child said that her mother had endured up until that point. When she found lice in the blankets she sat down and wept.

The first morning's chorus of Australian birdsong and the sunshine, even if chilly, was fully strange to the newcomers, particularly if they had been city-dwellers. All the sights, sounds and smells were utterly new for them. Kookaburras sounded outlandish. In our camp the kookaburras were known as 'Ha Ha Pigeons' and we had to instruct that not only were they not pigeons, they were not to be eaten.

As soon as possible, the newcomers were sorted and assigned to some sort of employment, in accordance with the original reason for their acceptance to our country. They were under a two-year bond to work in whatever capacity assigned them. Over their heads was the threat of instant repatriation back to Europe if there was any disagreement with the appointment. I never knew this threat to be effected. But it was there and could be invoked.

There were plenty more people waiting to step into a boat which would take them to a perceived golden land.

Some were sent immediately to employment. Those sent to camp or hostel and still segregated from their family suffered great inconvenience. One woman told me how she went to the Red Cross at the war's end to try to find her husband again after many years' separation. The Nazis has conscripted her husband into the Luftwaffe as a mechanic. Then at Somers he was put into dormitory-type accommodation. Eventually he was sent somewhere to pick grapes and she and the daughter went to a camp for women and children only. Most of the first ten years of their marriage, she and he lived apart. Only when they found their own house could they live as man and wife.

This matter of accommodation was problematic. The lack of language was a great hindrance to many. They were unsure of their rights, afraid to offend in case they were evicted. Very often the living quarters offered were expensive and substandard. Some gradually saved enough to buy, or at least put down a deposit on, a block of land, which gave them just that – a piece of land with The first morning's chorus of Australian birdsong and the sunshine, even if chilly, was fully strange to the newcomers, particularly if they had been city-dwellers. All the sights, sounds and smells were utterly new for them. Kookaburras sounded outlandish. In our camp the kookaburras were known as 'Ha Ha Pigeons' and we had to instruct that not only were they not pigeons, they were not to be eaten.

As soon as possible, the newcomers were sorted and assigned to some sort of employment, in accordance with the original reason for their acceptance to our country. They were under a two-year bond to work in whatever capacity assigned them. Over their heads was the threat of instant repatriation back to Europe if there was any disagreement with the appointment. I never knew this threat to be effected. But it was there and could be invoked.

There were plenty more people waiting to step into a boat which would take them to a perceived golden land.

Some were sent immediately to employment. Those sent to camp or hostel and still segregated from their family suffered great inconvenience. One woman told me how she went to the Red Cross at the war's end to try to find her husband again after many years' separation. The Nazis has conscripted her husband into the Luftwaffe as a mechanic. Then at Somers he was put into dormitory-type accommodation. Eventually he was sent somewhere to pick grapes and she and the daughter went to a camp for women and children only. Most of the first ten years of their marriage, she and he lived apart. Only when they found their own house could they live as man and wife.

This matter of accommodation was problematic. The lack of language was a great hindrance to many. They were unsure of their rights, afraid to offend in case they were evicted. Very often the living quarters offered were expensive and substandard. Some gradually saved enough to buy, or at least put down a deposit on, a block of land, which gave them just that – a piece of land with no roads, no water supply, no deep drainage, no electricity nor gas.

They had to virtually camp until they had saved more money to begin to erect a sort of humpy as a temporary dwelling.

In the cities, some families shared a house or an apartment to save on exorbitant rents. Quite often a whole family lived in one room, with or without children. All must share the kitchen, laundry, bathroom and toilet facilities. If ever there was a test of patience and cooperation, that surely must have been one.

Until accommodation had been secured, the families had to stay in camp, well beyond the six months sometimes. Obviously, those with the most get-up-and-go were the first to find both work and housing. They were also often the first to save enough for land or a house. Once they left, they were very much on their own. If they found themselves among good neighbours, they would be taken under the wing of the locals and in the first days there were centres of assistance such as the Good Neighbour Council, which was there to help those who sought help.

As I have said, building materials were hard to find. Houses were put together in ways which would be illegal these days. Everyone was desperate to put a roof over their head, whether local or migrant. Some built houses from packing cases in which European cars had been imported, from beautiful timber like cottonwood or beech.

One couple told me of how they lived in a garage until a house could be built. They had to dig their own toilet. They had no water, fridge, electricity or sewerage. There were eight children in this family. Initially they did without furniture. Even though they had no carpets nor lino, they did have curtains. Boxes served as tables and chairs. Theirs was no isolated case. It was repeated many times.

8 Migrants at Work

Work was decided by Australia: the sugar fields in Queensland, the Hydro Electric Scheme in Tasmania, the Commonwealth Railways, the General Post Office – workers were required everywhere. Lack of language was a hindrance. Most initial arrangements were made in German with an assisting interpreter. At that time very few government officials had a working knowledge of any language except English. Spoken English back then was of better quality than today's.

Some migrants tried to keep together in groups and sometimes this wish was granted. Maybe some official realised they would be happier and settle in quicker and easier if they could help each other. If the work was far from the camp, the men would be given a rail ticket and some money. They had to simply get on with their lives.

I obtained this statement from one man:

We arrived in Melbourne from Ballarat about the end of March and without any special welcome or ceremony were taken as the first ones to Broadmeadows Army camp, about 15 kilometres from the city. They called us Balts and there were only empty space around us... Our first task was to clean the barracks for ourselves, to move in beds, mattresses and bedding. Two or three Australian men would come every day to carry out maintenance.

We also washed floors, placed tables in the dining room, helped the cooks with the dishes and pots; lighted the fires in the kitchen stoves, fixing and cleaning the barracks for the incoming workers. We were even allotted a cart and a horse to carry out rubbish to the dump.

Little attention was given to the migrants' former training or experience. So we could have doctors and lawyers pushing trolleys or on farms. Some did manage to wheedle their way into more congenial positions, once they had summed up the situation.

Again:

> At noon as we found out from the PMG workers that they were getting £8 a week, some of us from the kitchen decided to change jobs but it was not easy as we had signed a two-year contract and so had to remain at the place of that contract...having another Pole as translator, we were able to convince the clerks that because both jobs were under the Commonwealth and that we were already a bit older (they had come as minors), they agreed and gave permission to us to move to the PMG and our weekly wage increased from £3 to £17.14.0.

Once the two-year bond had expired or they were released by one of the ever recurring strikes, they then could choose their own way. To many of the 'new Australians' the strikers and strikes and the go-slow tactics were incomprehensible and pointless. They conformed because they would be in strife if they baulked. To them it seemed that here there was no pride in work, no proper satisfaction in the finished product or effort. Those who had been trained in the old-style European standards of workmanship, reacted with anger, amazement, frustration and disappointment. But they were outnumbered and felt threatened.

However, if the strike were of long duration, they could demand to be released. Their weekly wage was an urgent necessity. They had no funds behind them to carry them over the hiatus. A long strike gave them an out and the opportunity to make their way independently.

Some professional people, whose qualifications had been refused because they were not British ones, were forced to repeat their entire studies in order to practise their profession. It is not easy to study when one is past one's youth. It is hard with few worldly goods behind one and hardest of all when a wife and a family have to be provided for. It is a puzzle that fraternal cooperation was not offered by like professionals and assistance given.

Yet, some did manage to overcome all obstacles. At what cost we will never know. They were then able to better serve their compatriots who were shy of consulting an Aussie professional who would not understand the applicants' needs or concerns.

As I have already said, jobs were plentiful. If both wife and husband went to work, they had a better chance to buy a block or to build their own home and kit it out. If a worker was in a factory, he possibly had little conversation in English. If he had to face the general public, he had to learn quick smart.

Those who were the most critical of the lack of English among the migrants were those who could not master a second language and who, maybe, did not speak their own correctly. Let us remember Australian English is not the best: too many mutter without moving their lips adequately. When I first went back into Australian schools, I had difficulty in understanding the mumblings of many children.

Because of their poor command of English, many migrants were doomed to continue in menial and poorly paid jobs. Some were happy to do so. It brought in a wage and a wage went towards the purchase of land or a house. The ownership of property gave the security of tenure to overcome the terrible losses from the war. Menial jobs were honest work, requiring little brain fag. When the worker finished for the day, he had no responsibility which could have been a drawback. After work there was a house to build, a garden to dig for self-sufficiency, children to care for. Moreover, many had two full-time jobs; one paid wages, the other gave income for saving.

If they worked all through the week, they tried to make Sunday truly a day of rest. The churchgoers could worship in their own languages and be with their own folk. It was an important social occasion giving refreshment from the alien environment which Monday workdays brought. One Russian woman told me that, after the drudgery of her workplace and of settling into a new life, she attended cultural events 'to feed her soul'.

9. Cultural Changes

The impact of new Australians on our cultural life can never be underestimated, especially regarding Sundays. The silence of our earlier Australian Sundays was completely in contrast to the migrants' former way of life.

The specialness of Sunday was impressed on me strongly as I grew up. That day was the Lord's Day and held to be holy, with no work, no merriment and no commercial enterprising allowed.

Activity was limited to emergencies, like police, fire fighting, ambulance driving. Churchgoing was the only outlet and twice a day was expected. In Melbourne, public transport was limited to one service per hour. Most shops, cafés, hotels were closed. Once the museum, art gallery or botanic gardens had been visited, after church attendance of course, there was little else to do.

One could see small migrant families, or single people, wandering the streets aimlessly, looking for something to do, someone to see. Sunday observance was maintained fanatically by the dogooders. Yet the strangers within our midst were there, lost and lonely, until some of the more enterprising of the café owners, who may have been earlier new arrivals, opened the doors of their café (like Café Scheherezade?) and filled a need.

Some migrants would have liked to visit friends. But the cost of travel was an amount that had to be put aside for the cost of a house. One had to balance needs and wants: did they mix with their own or save the cost of fares? How much longer were they to suffer unkind landlords or substandard accommodation? Remember, these people came with nothing except what they could carry. So they needed to begin at the very beginning, trying to then build up all that we take for granted. Everything costs money. Nothing falls from heaven to the place beneath – except, perhaps, mercy – but mercy was in short supply.

So then it was the eating places which were the first to realise that Sunday was not only a day of rest and gladness, but that the gladness would be more abundant if the newcomers were made comfortable and welcome – at a modest price. Food. Slowly, subtly the diet extended and enlarged as new foods came onto the market for the brave ones to sample. Once a shop or market stall offered some culinary variety, word went around and demand grew. Rarities became popular as Australians began to try, taste and like.

Gradually there sprang up eating places for ethnic groups. This is another new word, 'ethnic', not used before migrants arrived. Initially they were patronised by their compatriots but were slowly accepted into the Australian way. In those days, no one would have dreamt that people would one day be deciding which cuisine to sample: 'Shall we eat Italian tonight, or perhaps Chinese?' Greek, Italian, Chinese had been here all along but avoided until they became chic or, anew word, upmarket. In early migrant days these catered for the homesick singles who had a little more money to spend on themselves than the families, who cooked for themselves and saved every penny.

In my youth, spaghetti was a stopgap snack food, obtained from a tin and quite bland to taste. Nowadays it is part of a pasta cuisine and has garlic – that foreign ingredient that wogs and dagos use and we shunned. Fifty years later, it is on supermarket shelves and enjoyed as a healthy additive to many dishes.

Vegetarian food was dull, dull, dull, boiled and overcooked, thoroughly uninteresting. To be vegetarian was to fly in the face of convention and needed some kind of courage to cope with the offerings. Look at it now. Meals without meat are exciting and adventurous, nourishing and appealing.

The migrants in their homes cooked in the fashion their forebears had done. But it was Australians who learned by eating at the ethnic cafés and restaurants and adapting the new cuisine in their kitchens. It was a giant step forward.

In the early days of my married life, I used to prepare two dishes for invited guests. In case they did not like the Russian dish provided, there was a less unusual dish available. But I found that the Russian food was well received and all guests were happy with this fare. I kept the plain food for my elders. It is the younger generation who are more adventurous.

With so many public eating places in large centres catering for every cuisine under the sun, one would think that the old British habit of requiring fish and chips with cups of tea to be served might have lessened. British food is incapable of adjusting. Do the British fear raw foods?

One migrant lady told me in shocked tones that she could not understand the Australian habit of killing the unwanted bull calves instead of selling the meat as veal, which those from Europe appreciated. They eschewed mutton and lamb. They sought out veal. Chicken they sought out too. The growth of the table chicken industry can be traced to migrant demand.

Recently, while I was on a trip to Germany, one of our kind and generous hosts recounted to us the extent of his travels for his business: two days in France or Italy, three in Denmark or Poland and so on. However, if he went to Britain he made certain he was back in Germany by nightfall.

This struck me as being odd and so I asked, "Why hurry home from Britain? Was it the British antipathy to Germans, even so long after the war?'

'No,' he said, 'they have carrots, potatoes and green vegetables like we have. What do they do to them?'

I laughed and replied, 'They boil them to death.'

By bringing people out on Sundays to see more than museums and art galleries, worthy though that is, the enterprising ones among us did more than provide a cuppa for the lonely. Along with food for the soul, Australians learned about another way of life, a new outlook for living in a modern world. The shackles of restrictive Sabbath observances were shaken off. I think it was Heine who wrote,

Laughter is wholesome. God is not as dull as some people make out. Did he not make the kitten to chase its tail?

Using Sunday for more than simply religious observances has been slow in gaining general acceptance, as old habits die hard. Those who reject the trend in having more Sunday recreations need not join in. For those who appreciate the fact of the day of rest and gladness being more accessible, there are now many outlets that, not too long ago, would never have been countenanced. This can be traced back to the advent of new Australians fifty years ago.

10. I Become a New Australian

In our decision to marry, George and I brought down coals of fire on our heads, mostly from my family. I had never met any of his people who lived in Brisbane. Travel was not easy fifty years ago, even interstate travel. At first meeting with George one would assume that he was a true-blue Aussie, as I have already said. He slouched like a local, spoke like a local. He was fair-haired and blue-eyed, of average height and a little stocky in build. No distinguishing marks announced him as a foreigner. Perhaps to a discerning eye, the Slavic cast of his face may have been there. To my mother, and through her to others, one would have thought he was the Devil incarnate. In later years George was wont to remark that, before we married, he thought that mother-in-law jokes were funny.

We had much in common, enjoying ballet, films, social occasions with friends and the like. In those days, to find a man who enjoyed going to ballet was a real miracle. We went to see the new phenomena: foreign films were coming more readily onto our screens. I met his friends. He met mine. We went to church, mostly to his which I found awe inspiring. All those candles and all that incense. All the beautiful sung music. It was so different from the good old C of E that I had grown up with.

Mother disapproved of everything we did or planned. In the end, we decided to marry in both of our churches because we had an affinity to our own. I had sung in the choir in mine. George attended his regularly. This meant that one wedding was in Melbourne. Then we would fly to Brisbane for the second service on the next day, a Russian orthodox ritual under the crowns. As the years went by, my children must have tired of hearing me quote Russian custom that when one is married under crowns it means that the husband and wife are king and queen in their home and that the children must therefore obey them.

So now I had a Russian name. Not a difficult one, but foreign nonetheless. It was generally assumed that I was a foreigner and thus I was treated as one by members of the public. I experienced initial mistrust, then some kind of disbelief that I had married a foreigner. Then came varying responses: mostly disdain. But some folk were kinder and even interested to find out the how and the why of it. Some people tried to speak more clearly to me; some shouted; some congratulated me on the quality of my English, for which I never failed to thank them. Others tried to explain ordinary terms to me and were surprised when I accepted their ministrations so easily.

In our private lives we spent much of our time among the Russians. For George, it was his custom and for me a new world. At the time of our wedding in Brisbane when I first met his family I could see that it was his milieu. The family lived in an all Russian area, attended the Russian orthodox Church nearby and spoke Russian among themselves. It was a little world all of its own. I was a new arrival in the family. Far from treating me as mine had treated George, which I had feared all the way to Brisbane, I was treated as a long-lost sister returning to the fold. I could scarcely believe it. My gratitude never faltered through successive years.

I began lessons in Russian. My in-laws and George's friends applauded. Progress was initially slow and painful. If one marries a foreigner, one should learn the language in order not to miss out on the gossip. However, there was in reality more to it than that. I did not need to learn his language: I wanted to learn it. The Brisbane Russians had lived there for many years from the early thirties, when Japan started her conquest of mainland Asia. They all spoke good English. However, the Melbourne Russians were new Australians and they needed all the help they could find.

At first, in Melbourne, I had tried to communicate in my schoolgirl French. Most of those Russians had lived in France for many years. It was heavy going. At the end of a few hours' conversation, my jaws were aching from the unaccustomed use of the organs of speech that the French language demands. Gradually they learned a little more English and I a little more Russian.

Comprehension improved. I learned about their customs and superstitions. I learned to cook Russian food. I even learned to eat and enjoy sour cream. I went to church with them and kept up the feasts. Not the fasts, however, as I was unused to so much strict religious observance. In the end, my mother declared that I was more Russian than the Russians.

Our life together, apart from Mother's interference, was mostly pleasant. Sundays mornings we went to church, sometimes dined with friends and often went to the Russian club of a Sunday evening. The club gave music, dancing, singing and sometimes a 'Dutch auction ' was a fundraiser. As time went on and the people made a life for themselves, there would be a Russian ball, to which I frequently invited my schoolfriends and their husbands.

Everyone entered into the spirit of the occasion and had a good time. My friends enjoyed trying the foreign dishes I prepared and a cross-pollination of ideas proved beneficial to everyone. In time these friends were tempted to try dishes from other sources, a trend which spread over Australia at varying rates of progress.

Among the Russians I was a sort of go-between in that I was the one to try and explain our Australian way of life, which puzzled them. In many cases I really needed to scratch my brains a bit to question for myself, the why of some of the things we took for granted in daily life. They were fascinated by our small, individual houses. In Europe in better times people lived in apartment buildings, in their own flats. One lady lived with her family in a 700-year-old French castle, wherein they had their apartment. To some it seemed that Australians lived in dolls' houses. Sunday observance was ludicrous to them. They went to church and, after that, Sunday was the day of socialising before the Monday grind. Bear in mind that many had any job that they could obtain in order to rebuild their lives, regardless of their previous training. Employment to many gave no job satisfaction. They needed the money and had to bear it with such grace as they could muster. Their condition brought slights and misunderstandings.

George was able to help with translations. There were not the multilingual brochures and notices that now abound in most cities. Back then, if you didn't speak English, mate, too bad. You had better learn it. Trying to work out forms and government by laws and the like was terribly difficult for many migrants. Some were too afraid of rebuffs and rejections to ask for help outside their national groups.

Postscript

This is the point at which Marina's manuscript ends. It sounds unfinished. No doubt she intended to write more, one day... But what she has left us gives an insight into the strange world of those who came to this country after World War II. They were the brave forerunners of successive groups, like the Vietnamese, the Cambodians, the Lebanese and, more recently, the refugees from Chad.

Beverley Marion Lutz-Dyer married George Volkoff in November 1951, in Jolimont, Melbourne, on 2 November and then in Brisbane in George's family church with a Russian Orthodox service on 25 November. A daughter, Margarita, followed in July 1953. The marriage did not last and she remarried and had three children: a son, Romann, in April 1958; another daughter, Kira, in October 1961; and her last, Matvei, a son, in 1966. George died on New Year's Eve in 1973 and Marina herself on 26 September 2005. There are now six grandchildren, four boys and two girls. Her influence spreads far wider than her family – evidence of a born teacher.

Marina wrote the following letter to her daughter on 26 April 1976. It reveals much that is admirable about Marina: her respect for and love of children in general and of her daughter in particular; her philosophy of teaching, which encompassed an understanding of the power of the teacher, a deep dedication to the wise use of this power and a reverence for learning.

> I am quite concerned that you are only 'just' alive – and feel that the root base of it all is much more than ordinary run of the mill work. I don't know what they taught you for five years in uni but I do know what they did NOT and that is the key to your present attitude to your job and your inability to cope with your situation.

Because of you (and some others in our schools) I have cast my mind back over the long years and remember my first year out – it was fun, it was exhilarating – it was also Hard Work but we had such a zest in tackling it and such a sense of achievement in rising up to the new demands made on us. I feel that the young ones are missing out badly on a great experience and have to fathom WHY. And all I can come up with is the fact that you have not been fitted for your job – not trained.

Firstly we were taught to teach. We read old Elijah (E.J., Principles and Techniques of Teaching) till we knew it almost by heart, we studied education history and methods of teaching but we were intended teachers so as teachers we were trained. Shown what to teach, various methods of attack, shortcomings thereof, other variants possible, how to deal with naughty ones, what to do, what not to do (a lot of time given to this – and kids then were far better brought up than these poor neglected monsters now are), how to cope with admin in all its multifarious forms – even about cleaning loos!

As far as I can gather, your Dip Ed is very little more than vague essays and lectures on theory and grey dreams of education in general. I may be wrong – 1 am an expert on that! – but that's the impression I gained. Teaching is one of the most demanding, challenging and rewarding jobs in the world, did they tell you that? I say you need to be a whole person to cope – NOT perfect – you must have one or two little foibles for the kids to poke at! But you must be whole – wholly confident, wholly humble, wholly serviceable (see Chaucer!) and, above all, wholly loving (see I Cor. 13). You must love them, dirty noses and all, or quit teaching and go work at Coles or Woolworths. I don't cuddle their poor stinking little bodies – in government teaching it is best not to lay a hand on them in anger or in care – it can be misconstrued – but kids know when you love them enough to care that they are well, are doing well, are happy.

If you are in pieces inside, you must walk into every class with a calm happy smile on your face. If you can put that one over successfully, you are halfway there – smile as if you are happy with them for that forty minutes or twice that, but smile. They will be your mirror. They reflect your attitude all the way and sometimes it can be that few realise it: even the oldies are blind in this too often. A teacher stands in loco parentis and in far too many cases has more power than the parents. (I quote from Form 3 at Girton and the question of the bikinis that Mum wouldn't pay $15 to buy!) The power is in your hands for better or for worse – whichever way you use it determines OUR futures, for these children are the ones to make our old age – or the alternative! It is no longer the hand that rocks the cradle which rules the nation for far too many mothers have abrogated their rights along with their responsibilities and no longer rear their children, they reproduce (any fool can do that), but after bringing these poor brats into the world abandon them thereto to go out and earn more coin for luxuries. All that children need is TLC in large doses. This they are not getting from so many parents, and here is where your power comes in. All teachers have it – but how is it being used? Do you have enough conviction of what is right and what is not? Things which are not right are not necessarily wrong, but still they are not right – what do you support? Children have a keen sense of rightness and justice, which must be nurtured and guided. That they do not live up to it only underlines the fact that their elders must do so in order to guide the young aright. That they do not is shown in the current hedonistic way of life.

You do not need to be a popular teacher, but you need to be absolutely just. This with proper respect for them and for your own principles will endure far better than mere popularity.

I get carried away with this as you well know but teaching the young is so terribly, frighteningly important that I feel that if you are not putting all you have into it – all you have of love (TLC), of enthusiasm, of joie de vivre, of wisdom (which can only come with years and years), then pay your bond and be quit of it. You must have a happy attitude and love your job, your kids and even the challenge of your problems – or get out. That I feel you are not really on top of it I blame on the system; you are only one of many victims, but you are mine own and I do love you so much and want so much that you will be happy in your chosen field that I speak as I have done.

www.ingramcontent.com/pod-product-compliance
Lightning Source LLC
Chambersburg PA
CBHW062204100526
44589CB00014B/1948